FAITH A. OYEDEPO

The Spirit Of Faith

THE SPIRIT OF FAITH

Contents

INTRODUCTION

Abel, Noah, Abraham, Isaac, Jacob, Moses, David, Jesus, and Paul, as well as dozens of other great men of Bible times all had one thing in common: the spirit of faith. They had operating in them an unusual grace, a peculiar unction that made it possible for them to do exploits. That singular quality caused them to please God.

Faith is a familiar subject to many full gospel believers. But there is another dimension to the faith message: the possessing of the spirit of faith. It was this spirit operating in Abel that made him offer a more excellent sacrifice than Cain, because he believed that God was not unjust to demand for a sacrifice. Thus by faith, he presented his gift to God, knowing that He is a rewarder, not a collector. Also possessing the spirit of faith, Enoch walked with God, disappointing death and experiencing a translation.

In these perilous times in which we live, it will take more than a head knowledge of the subject of faith to be translated above hardship. It will take being filled with the spirit of faith. It is operating in this spirit that will cause you to "arise and shine" inspite of the gross darkness that will cover the present world system. It is by crying out for this spirit that the abundance of the sea shall be converted unto you.

Suddenly, like the faith generals in Hebrews 11, you too will be enabled to subdue kingdoms, obtain promises, stop the mouth of lions, quench the violence of fires, escape the edge of the sword, wax valiant in fight and turn to flight the armies of the aliens. Operating in the spirit of faith you will receive your dead back to life again and obtain a good report.

Wherever the spirit of faith is operational, nothing is impossible to the possessor. You become a bona fide child of God and a co-creator with your heavenly Father, because:

> ***"Through faith we understand that the worlds were framed by the word of God, so that things which are seen were not made of things which do appear."***
>
> *Hebrews 11:3*

Walking in the same spirit of faith you can frame your world to your taste. You enter into the realm where "you have it the way you want it."

Shadrach, Meshach, and Abednego had more than just a head knowledge of the subject of faith; they entered into a realm where they could be described as "faith drunk". King Nebuchadnezzar commanded them to bow down in worship of his golden image or else they will be thrown into a burning fiery furnace. The "faith drunk" men replied undisturbed:

> ***"… O Nebuchadnezzar, we are not careful to answer thee in this matter.***
>
> ***If it be so, our God whom we serve is able to deliver us from the burning fiery furnace, and he will deliver us out of thine hand, O king, But if not, be it known unto thee, O king, that we will not serve thy gods …"***
>
> Daniel 3:16-18

Furious and in a wild rage, Nebuchadnezzar heated up the furnace seven times more, then threw Shadrach, Meshach, and Abednego into it. The result was, they felt no hurt! The fire had no power over their bodies! Their secret? They possessed the spirit of faith. You too can become an impossible case to the devil, if you will just desire the spirit of faith. You don't have to live at the mercy of the enemy anymore. You have what it takes to put ten thousand devils to flight!

The times we live in are the times when all around us is burning like an oven heated seven times. Financial ovens, ovens in the family, ovens in businesses; but with a full dose of the spirit of faith, you will be distinguished. It doesn't matter how hot the world burns, what will make a difference are those who are serving God with this spirit of faith.

The Spirit Of Faith

"We having the same spirit of faith, according as it is written, I believed, and therefore have I spoken; we also believe, and therefore speak."

II Corinthians 4:13

From the above quoted scripture, we understand that the substance called faith has a spirit. It has something akin to the petrol in a car. That is, faith, like wisdom, understanding, counsel, might, knowledge and the fear of God (described in Isaiah 11:2) has a spirit. It has a fuel, a driving force, something of a supernatural qualification that keeps it going. When Moses laid his hands on Joshua, what came upon him

9

was not just wisdom, but the spirit of wisdom (Deut. 34:9). Filled with this spirit, Joshua did untold exploits.

Is the spirit of faith a unique spirit from God? From observing the use of similar expressions like "the spirit of adoption", "the spirit of Christ", the spirit of glory", "spirit of grace", "spirit of knowledge", spirit of meekness", "spirit of promise", "spirit of prophecy", "spirit of truth", "spirit of understanding", and "spirit of wisdom", it is possible to deduce that all these are different manifestations of the Spirit of God, the Holy Spirit. He is the Spirit of adoption, the Spirit of Christ, etc. He is also in essence the Spirit of faith.

The Holy Spirit who has been right from the beginning of time was the fuel behind the faith of Abel, Abraham, Moses, David, and Jesus. This may account for the similarity in results. In Old Testament times the Holy Spirit could not indwell the Israelites. He only came upon a select few to enable them perform their divine assignments. That was why Moses needed to lay hands on Joshua to impart upon him the spirit of wisdom that was operational in his own life. Samuel also had to anoint David before the Spirit of God could come upon him and equip him to rule over God's people. Perhaps someone may ask, "Could II Corinthians

4:13 be referring to the Holy Spirit as the Spirit of faith, considering that the spirit referred to is written with a small letter 's'?" I believe it still refers to the Spirit of God, because in Isaiah 11:2, the "spirit" used there is also written in small letter "s", yet it is evidently the Spirit of God that was to come upon Jesus and fill Him with knowledge, understanding, wisdom, counsel, and the fear of God.

As a natural man you have natural faith. You do not need to be born again to sit down on a chair. You simply believe that if you sit on the chair in your parlour it will carry your weight. You may or may not understand how an airplane works, yet to travel by air, you board an aircraft and sit in it by faith, believing that you would arrive at your destination. That is natural faith.

But even natural faith involves acting on what you believe. Do you believe that the chair can carry your weight? You say "yes" by sitting on it. Thus, the evidence that you believe is your acting on what you believe.

When you get born-again, at that instance you receive a measure of the Spirit of God.

> **"... No man can say that Jesus is the Lord, but by the Holy Ghost."**
>
> I Corinthians 12:3

11

That little measure of the Spirit of God you receive at salvation is what imparts the faith to believe God for answers to prayer, financial supplies, etc. But on the day you get baptized in the Holy Ghost, you are immersed into Him; you are filled to overflowing.

"...According as God hath dealt to every man <u>the measure of faith.</u>"

Romans 12:3

"He that believeth on me as the scripture hath said, out of his belly shall flow rivers of living water. (But this spake he of the Spirit, which they that believe on him should receive ...)".

John 7:38, 39

To further establish this assertion, let's consider the man Peter. The moment he accepted to follow Jesus, he was born-again. In fact, with his mouth he confessed that Jesus is the Christ, the Messiah, the Son of God (Matthew 16:16). Peter, therefore, had a measure of the spirit of faith. That was why when Jesus was walking on water and beckoned on him to do likewise, Peter quickly responded. He took a step of faith! However, to prove that it was just a small measure of faith he had, Peter soon began to sink (Matthew 14:28-31). With the measure of faith he had, Peter could not stand up in defense of Jesus, but denied Him thrice in quick successions (Luke 22:55-61). But when the day of Pentecost was fully come, however, the failing faith of Peter received a shot of heavenly adrenaline (Acts 2:4,14)! He could now face the Sanhedrin fearlessly, declaring that Jesus is Lord! Peter also had the faith to heal a man that had been lame for forty years (Acts 3:1-9).

If you are born-again, you have a measure of the spirit of faith. You have the capability to act on the Word of God, because of the Holy Spirit within you, who helps you.

MEASURES OF THE SPIRIT OF FAITH

"And when the man that had the line in his hand went forth eastward, he measured a thousand cubits, and he brought me through the waters; the waters were to the ankles".

Ezekiel 47:3

Ankle deep is the first measure of the spirit of faith. It is the measure of faith a man has when he surrenders his life to Jesus. It is the Holy Spirit who places in his heart enough faith to believe that he can become a child of God simply by inviting Jesus into his heart. If the Spirit of God does not impart this measure of faith, it would be impossible for a man to accept that by just believing in his heart and confessing with his mouth the Lord Jesus, he becomes a new creature. The work of grace is effective through faith, which is imparted by the Holy Spirit.

"For by grace are ye saved through faith ..."

Ephesians 2:8

Thus, at repentance, the spirit of faith enables you to believe and voice out that belief.

"We having the same spirit of faith, according as it is written, I believed, and therefore have I spoken ..."

II Corinthians 4:13

For instance, when Paul had that heavenly visitation in which Jesus spoke to him asking, "Saul, Saul, why persecutest thou me?" Paul responded to that "altar call" by asking "Who art thou, Lord?" It was the "ankle deep" measure of the spirit of faith that moved him to acknowledge Jesus as Lord. He could have rebuffed the voice and scoffed at the instructions, but he believed that Jesus is Lord and yielded to the divine instruction to *"Arise, and go into the city, and it shall be told thee what thou must do"* (Acts 9:1-6).

I believe it is not far-fetched to interpret Ezekiel 47 this way, because when you step into a stream, the water is not instantly at your waist level, but at your ankle. Similarly, when you step into the Christian faith, your first contact with the spirit of faith is ankle deep; it is the ability to acknowledge Jesus as Lord.

"Again he measured a thousand, and brought me through the waters; the waters were to the knees ..."
Ezekiel 47:4

The **knee-deep** level of the spirit of faith refers to a higher dimension of this grace. Many people who refuse to graduate from the ankle deep level find that despite their zeal to serve God, they are limited. This reminds me of some missionaries who died of starvation while on the mission field. They were sincere Christians, but lacked the knowledge and faith to cause food to come on their tables. Perhaps all they had was the ankle deep measure of the spirit of faith, so they were heaven ready, and thus went before their time.

When you are baptized in the Holy Ghost, you are knee-deep in the spirit of faith. You are filled with power - power for evangelism, power to cast out devils, to take up serpents and not be hurt, power not to be hurt by any deadly thing, and power to lay your hands on the sick and see them recover.

"But ye shall receive power, after that the Holy Ghost is come upon you; and ye shall be witnesses unto

me both in Jerusalem, and in all Judaea, and in Samaria, and unto the uttermost part of the earth."

Acts 1:8

There was a man named Apollos, a Jew born in Alexandria. The Bible records that he was an eloquent man, mighty in the scriptures and zealous. However, having only an ankle-deep measure of the spirit of faith, he was limited. True, he spoke boldly, teaching diligently; but those who heard him (like Priscilla and Aquila), being aware of a deeper dimension of the spirit, had to take him aside and minister to him. But when he went deeper in the spirit, he provided more help to the brethren and had a higher rate of success at soul winning (you can read the full account in Acts 18:24-28).

"... Again he measured a thousand; and brought me through; the waters were to the loins."

Ezekiel 47:4

Loin-deep: This is greater than the ankle-deep and knee-deep measure. It signifies the operation of the spirit of faith in a man which is higher than at new birth and the baptism. A clear illustration of this is in Acts 4. In Acts 2 there was the outpouring of the Holy Ghost; it was the baptism of the Holy Spirit. But in Acts 4, the apostles gathered and prayed, asking for the anointing of the Holy Spirit. What did they want to see accomplished?

> *"... Grant unto thy servants, that with all boldness they may speak thy word, By stretching forth thine hand to heal; and that signs and wonders may be done by the name of thy holy child Jesus.*
>
> *And when they had prayed, the place was shaken where they were assembled together; and they were all filled with the Holy Ghost, and they spake the word of God with boldness."*
>
> Acts 4:29-31

They wanted greater boldness to declare the word and greater signs and wonders done through them.

The anointing is subsequent to baptism. With the anointing you receive a greater percentage of power. You enter into the "great power" and "great grace" level.

> *"And with <u>great power</u> gave the apostles witness of the resurrection ... and <u>great grace</u> was upon them all."*
>
> *Acts 4:33*

As a result of this, lack and want died a permanent death in their lives. It is the anointing that helps you exercise faith at sonship level. That is, as a son, not a baby or an infant, you are enabled to manifest your sonship. Power is released to make performance possible.

The anointing empowers you to act on God's Word and to see results of your faith. Whatever your calling or area of service, loin-deep in the spirit of faith brings you a high level of accomplishment. Whether as a layman or a minister of the gospel, your faith level is upped when you are anointed by the Holy Ghost. You become a yoke-breaking, mountain-moving, demon-destroying Christian. You win, not by power or struggles any longer, but cheaply by the Holy Spirit.

Paul, after his conversion and baptism in the Holy Ghost, still went to Arabia to commune with God and receive the unction for a hitch-free ministry. The spirit of faith was so operational in his life that special miracles were wrought by the anointing through handkerchiefs and aprons (Acts 19:12).

> *"Afterward he measured a thousand; and it was a river that I could not passover: for the waters were risen, waters to swim in, a river that could not be passed over."*
>
> Ezekiel 47:5

A River-Level measure of the spirit of faith is still the anointing, but describes a greater depth of the anointing. From this we realize that even though you are anointed, increase in that anointing is possible. We are not all at the same level of anointing; some are at a point where the waters are risen so much that it is as if they are living in a different world. They are translated like Enoch. The miracles Jesus and some of the apostles did show they were at this level of the spirit of faith.

Jonathan Edwards, D. L. Moody, Charles Finney, Kathryn Kuhlman, the Jeffrey Brothers, and Smith Wigglesworth, to mention just a few, swam in an unusual anointing of the Holy Spirit. An instance of the display of tremendous faith came when a man died in the audience when Smith Wigglesworth was preaching.

"Pick him up!" Wigglesworth said. Then he punched the dead man in the stomach, as the story goes, and said, sternly, "In Jesus' name, rise!" But the man was still dead. "Pick him up again!" he commanded, even more sternly. "I said, in Jesus' name, rise!" Nothing happened. "Let him go." Still the man was dead and fell to the floor, and for the third time, he directed that the man be picked up. "I said, in Jesus' name, rise!" And this time, he slapped the man in the face. This time, the man opened his eyes: he was alive!

That is the river-level measure of the spirit of faith.

You can do great exploits this end-time, if only you will ask the Holy Spirit to fill you with the spirit of faith.

ACCESS TO THE SPIRIT OF FAITH

What you need in order to have an access to this Spirit is a thirst for it.

> *"Ho, everyone that <u>thirsteth</u>, come ye to the waters, and he that hath no money; come ye, buy, and eat; yea, come, buy <u>wine</u> and <u>milk</u> without money and without price."*
>
> Isaiah 55:1

> *The wine and milk spoken about talks of the Spirit of God. The Bible says: "... Be not drunk with wine, wherein is excess; but be filled with the <u>Spirit</u>"*
> *(Ephesians 5:18).*

You can be filled with the spirit of faith to the point where just at your appearance mountains are leveled. However, the above scripture tells us the pathway to gaining access into that overflowing:

A Thirst

"Ho, everyone that <u>thirsteth,</u> come ..." There has to be a thirst, a craving or longing. *"... Without money ..."* The spirit of faith cannot be purchased

20

with money, but with a genuine thirst - a thirst for God, a thirst to see Him move through you in a greater way. Don't be satisfied with the level of faith you are operating in now. No! There is yet a higher level you can attain. David said:

"As the hart panteth after the water brooks, so panteth my soul after thee, O God."

Psalm 42:1

He was constantly panting after God, for a greater experience in God. If you want to experience an increase, an infilling of the spirit of faith, *"thirst"* is the key, because it is only after a thirsting that you can be filled (Matthew 5:6).

Each time you ask for an infilling, God checks your heart to see whether there is a real thirst for it, or whether you are merely asking because everyone else is asking. Look at your life, examine yourself, have you accepted the status quo? Has the enemy deceived you by saying you can do nothing about your situation? Or do you feel you have arrived; there is no greater glory than where you are? Thinking any of these thoughts will cause you to accept the ordinary, instead of God's best. Don't be robbed of God's best; be thirsty for more of God.

Paul the apostle, despite his many revelations and

visitations to the heavenlies, craved for more of God.

> **"That I may know him, and the power of his resurrection ..."**
>
> Philippians 3:10

You can't afford to think you know it all (II Corinthians 8:2). Thank God for where you presently are in the spirit, but there is still a better place ahead you need to get to.

To be able to thirst for the spirit of faith sincerely, you need to acknowledge your emptiness and insufficiency. Your experience of new birth and the Holy Ghost baptism are just a start, they are just the beginning. Like my husband often says, *"registration does not mean graduation."* That you have registered in the kingdom of God as a born again child of God and baptized in the Spirit, does not equal graduation (manifestation of your sonship in God). There needs to be a pressing forward.

To press forward in the spirit of faith, recognize how much you need Him on a daily basis. The Bible says: *"Without me (Jesus) ye can do nothing"* (John 15:5). This helps you to see the utter hopelessness of challenging mountains, obstacles, and situations without the spirit of faith.

Ask

After a thirst comes the asking. Ask for the filling of the spirit of faith. It is not just enough to be thirsty, you need to ask for a filling.

> *"... Whatsoever ye shall <u>ASK</u> the Father in my name, he will give it you. Hitherto have he <u>asked</u> nothing in my name: <u>ask</u>, and ye shall receive that your joy may be full."*
>
> John 16:23, 24

Express your thirst for the spirit of faith by asking for it in prayer; and because it is the will of God for your faith to be on the increase, He will grant your request.

Jesus' disciples said: *"Lord, Increase our faith" (Luke 17:5)*. The spirit of faith can be on the increase in your life. All you need do is, out of a thirsty heart, ask the Lord for it, and your request shall be granted. *"Ask, and it shall be given you" (Matthew 7:7)*.

Your praying in the Holy Ghost with other tongues is a vital part in the process of asking for the spirit of faith, because God's words tells us that:

> *"Likewise the Spirit also helpeth our infirmities: for we know not what we should pray for as we ought: but the Spirit itself maketh intercession for us with groanings which cannot be uttered.*

And he that searcheth the hearts knoweth what is the mind of the Spirit, because he maketh intercession for the saints according to the will of God."

Romans 8:26-27

This tells us that when we engage the Holy Spirit by praying in other tongues, we are actually praying the very will of God into manifestation, and rooting out the obstacles in the way.

Praying in the Holy Ghost or speaking in tongues also edifies or builds you up. It develops and strengthens your spirit man (1 Corinthians 14:4; Jude 20). As you begin to pray in tongues you become changed, and the Holy Spirit goes to work, causing you to be a channel for the flow of the spirit of faith.

Two

Components Of
The Spirit Of Faith

"We having the same spirit of faith, according as it is written, I believed, and therefore have I spoken; we also believe, and therefore speak."

II Corinthians 4:13

The spirit of faith has two major components or qualities: belief and speaking. These are two things without which you cannot claim to possess the spirit of faith. There must be a belief, then bold declarations.

"I Believed ..."

Whatever the word of God says, the spirit of faith dares to believe. He helps you to stand firm upon the word of God, to hope against hope. That is, even when the situation appears hopeless, you can hold on firmly to God's word. You, therefore, need to search the scriptures for a guarantee, and believe what the Word says.

> *"... If thou canst believe, all things are possible to him that believeth."*
>
> Mark 9:23

Don't write off any situation as being hopeless. By believing God those trials will be turned to testimonies. At 75, Abraham was instructed by God to leave his hometown and head for a city which God would show him. It seemed incredible, but Abraham believed God. Sarah, aged and accustomed to her people, agreed to follow Abraham. She had confidence in the leadership of her husband, and him in the leadership of God.

> *"And he (Abraham) believed in the Lord; and he counted it to him for righteousness."*
>
> Genesis 15:6

When God saw the manifestation of the spirit of

faith in Abraham and Sarah, He could no longer keep His resting arms crossed, but intervened in their lives. May be all that God is waiting for, to come to your rescue is belief.

Jesus entered into Capernaum, and there a centurion met Him, and beseeched Him to heal his servant, who was lying sick at home. The centurion expressed faith in Jesus' spoken word, and to him Jesus said: *"Go thy way; and as thou hast believed, so be it done unto thee"* (Matthew 8:13).

The Psalmist said he had fainted unless he had believed to see the goodness of the Lord in the land of the living (Psalms 27:13). Often we do the reverse: we want to see before we believe. The goodness of the land you live in has been reserved for you since the foundation of the earth; but to eat of it, you must first believe.

Isaiah the prophet lamented thus:

> **"Who hath believed our report? and to whom is the arm of the Lord revealed?"**
>
> *Isaiah 53:1*

The report of God is superior to the report of the doctor or the world. Has the world declared you a failure? That's the world's report. God says you are the head in your business. However, before it becomes a reality, you must believe it and allow it to cancel out the world's report.

A Science and Technology student noticed an unusual pain in his abdominal region. Taken to the University College Hospital (UCH), Ibadan, he was diagnosed as having cancer of the blood, leukemia. The disease being incurable, he was placed in a ward for critical cases. Daily people died around him. When he returned home to Lagos, the people of God began praying for him and he noticed an improvement.

However, he soon developed a cough, which caused pain in his sides, shoulders and armpit. He attended one of our church services. When the church service started he was unable to stand. But as the Bishop said he wanted to see each sick person healed, this young brother asked his parents to help him up. He later released himself and discovered he could stand and turn around, things he could not do before. The symptoms of the disease vanished!

By believing the report of God, that Jesus Himself took our infirmities and bore our sickness, the doctor's report was canceled!

*"... **Blessed is she (or he) that believet:; for there***

shall be a performance of those things which were told her from the Lord."

Luke 1:45

What are the things God has told you in His word? If you dare to believe them, then there will be a performance for you. It doesn't matter how hard they may appear; God is the God of what man calls "impossible".

God has all-round rest for you, including financial and marital. But to enter that state of perpetual tranquility, you must possess the visa of belief. Only those who believe are qualified to enter God's rest.

"For we which have believed do enter into rest ..."

Hebrews 4:3

Do you desire a home patterned after Eden, where your wife is sweet and your husband loving? That's rest in the family. It is attainable as you believe the word and act out your part.

Christians are called believers because our profession is believing. We are called to a life of belief. We must believe in the Lord our God so that He can establish His promises in our lives (II Chronicles 20:20).

"... Therefore Have I Spoken"

The spirit of faith is not a dumb spirit; it speaks.

What you believe with your heart must proceed out of your mouth, or else there's no proof that you possess the spirit of faith. If you talk chaff, how can you expect to reap wheat? God is committed to giving you what you declare with your mouth.

"Say unto them, As truly as I live, saith the Lord, as ye have spoken in mine ears, so will I do to you."
Numbers 14:28

This passage points to the importance of speaking the right things. Do you confess defeat? No wonder defeat and failure hang around you. What you have occurring in your life right now is a result of what you keep saying. Change those negative statements to positive ones, and you will eat the good of the land.

"Say ye to the righteous, that it shall be well with him; for they shall eat the fruit of their doings."
Isaiah 3:10

God was tired of a blank, empty and shapeless world, so He declared what He wanted, and He saw what He said. Before the people began constructing the tower of Babel, they called themselves together and declared that they would build a tower, which would reach to heaven (Genesis 11:4).

The spirit of faith is manifested as you boldly declare

what you believe. The mountains of your life and the strangers are waiting to hear your voice. Jesus said, *"If you shall say to this mountain, be removed and be cast into the sea it shall be so"* (Matthew 21:21). Whether the mountains move or stay is dependent on what you say.

"Death and life are in the power of the tongue ..."
Proverbs 18:21

"Thou art snared with the words of thy mouth, thou art taken with the words of thy mouth."
Proverbs 6:2

A snare is a trap. So you can either be trapped or loosed by the words of your mouth. God has given you all things that you require for life and godliness, but your mouth is the spiritual sickle with which you harvest those promises. You must express your faith by the words of your mouth before it will produce. As you declare the word of God to the strangers of poverty, disease, and failure lurking around you, the strangers will fade out of their hiding places (Psalm 18:44,45).

When you speak the word, you demonstrate your deep conviction or belief that the word of God works. Any thing that is contrary to God's best for your life, don't keep watching it; clear it out of your way by speaking to it.

A woman from Niger state of Nigeria shared this testimony: She had an internal problem which had necessitated surgery twice. She was told to wait for a number of years before attempting to conceive. Her ears were full of the doctor's diagnosis. When she got home she heard a voice within her spirit-man asking, *"That was what the doctor said. What do you say?"* She replied: *"I don't want to be barren, I want to be a mother, I want to have a child."* She went before a mirror and declared: *"You woman in this mirror, you are not barren; all the wounds inside you are healed. You are able to conceive and bear your own baby, irrespective of what the doctor has said. You are a mother!"*

On getting to church a few days later, her pastor moved by the Spirit said, *"It doesn't matter what the doctors have told you, you are a mother!"* She believed and went home, all the while declaring the same words to herself over and over before her mirror. Shortly after, she became pregnant.

When her gynecologist learnt of the development he was worried. He informed her that she had made a fatal mistake. Her relatives began crying, anticipating the worst. Rather than despairing, she would go over to her mirror each time and declare, *"Woman it is well with you* (Isaiah 3:10)." When her pastor saw her again he prophesied "The child is going to be a boy, and his name will be Joseph."

As her time for delivery approached, no doctor would risk delivering her of the baby. At a point, fear crept into her heart and the devil said to her, "you will die." But she silenced the devil, saying, *"Long life is my portion. I shall not die, but live to declare the glory of God."* Well, this sister had a safe delivery against all odds, and it was truly a boy, whom they named Joseph.

Your present challenge is waiting to hear you exercise your authority through the words of your mouth. In the army, a general does not take orders from a sergeant. It is the reverse. Also, the general does not address the sergeant weakly and trembling. He commands the sergeant as one having authority over him. You have authority over the situations of your life. You have been given dominion over them all. So, speak to those issues as one conscious of your authority.

David knew that humanly speaking he could not defeat Goliath. But he was filled with the spirit of faith. His brothers could not understand him, they thought he was proud. They did not understand that he was 'drunk' with the spirit of faith. He was operating from a higher frequency when he said:

"This day will the Lord deliver thee into mine hand ..."

I Samuel 17:46

As he made this declaration boldly, Goliath's head was already chopped off in the realm of the spirit. My husband often says, *"A soundless Christian is a sign-less Christian."* You can get positive results in every-day life when you say positive things based on the word of God. So, frame your world, create a heaven on earth for yourself by what you say.

When you keep saying, *"I don't have"*, *"I cannot do it"*, *"I am sick"*, you cripple the spirit of faith. The spirit of faith is released by speaking the word of God. According to Mark 11:23, the mountains (obstacles) of your life will be moved if you would only activate the spirit of faith in you. Several believers keep their mouths shut and their hearts shouting in protest. They complain within. But rather than saying what they want, they keep sealed lips. No! Your mouth is a creative tool, not an instrument for gossip or mur-muring.

<u>Your Words Are Seeds</u>

When you speak a word, it is a spiritual seed, bound to germinate and produce after its kind. You don't plant maize and expect to reap wheat. No! The law of nature demands that you reap what you sow (Genesis 8:22).

What many are reaping today, such as barrenness, unemployment, sickness, weakness, and broken-heartedness, are a harvest of what they spoke yesterday. When you sow two grains of maize, what you reap is not just two grains. It's approximately four hundred grains per cob. If you want to reap long life, sow the word of God on long life; declare that you cannot die. Declare that a thousand and one people in your neighborhood may be attacked, but not you. When you sow good seeds, when others are reaping chaff, you will be reaping wheat.

> *"For the Lord spake thus to me with a strong hand, and instructed me that I should not walk in the way of this people, saying, Say ye not, A confederacy, to all them to whom this people shall say, A confederacy; neither fear ye their fear, nor be afraid.*
>
> *Sanctify the Lord of host himself; and let him be your fear, and let him be your dread."*
>
> Isaiah 8:11-13

God is still speaking with a strong voice to as many

as would listen. Don't say what others are saying, so you don't see what they're seeing. No matter how costly garri (a derivative from cassava) gets, don't join your colleagues in the office to complain. Even if it becomes 100 naira per cup, you cannot lack. If others say, *"Who can survive in Nigeria?"* say, *"Me"*. Others may term it as pride or indifference, but you know what you are doing. Don't fear their fear.

Fear is a spirit. It is the arch enemy of the spirit of faith. You must fight fear as a man fights an assailant. It's that serious! Job never knew failure or sickness, until he permitted the spirit of fear (Job 3:25). You cannot be possessed with faith and fear at the same time. If you're filled with fear, then faith is not there. If you operate in the spirit of faith, it chases away the spirit of fear.

Your Words Commits God

God thinks good thoughts about you, but they remain mere thoughts until you begin to declare them.

> *"Put me in remembrance: let us plead together: declare thou that thou mayest be justified."*
>
> Isaiah 43:26

God never forgets, yet He wants you to remind Him of His words. A paradox? Hardly! For instance, a father naturally knows what the needs of his child are. But when the child presents his desire before his father and keeps reminding him, even to the point of pestering, the father rushes to buy the item for the boy, if only to have some peace. Remember the parable of the widow and the unjust judge. The Bible says though he feared neither God nor man, *"yet because this widow troubleth me, I will avenge her, lest by her continual coming she weary me"* (Luke 18:5).

This was the unjust judge. How much more would God the Righteous Judge avenge you of your enemy of sickness, poverty, failure, etc., when you present your case before Him. However, to gain quick access verse 8 of the same reference says:

"... Nevertheless when the Son of man cometh, shall he find faith on the earth?"

Faith is what moves God into action. Faith in His word, loaded in the heart, and triggered by the mouth releases unprecedented breakthroughs.

Some Christians, however, make a habit of speaking contrary to what God's Word says, and as a result, God allows what has been spoken to happen. An example of this is the Israelites in the wilderness. They refused to believe the word of God, but instead began to murmur, complain, and give room to speaking evil.

And the Lord said, *"As truly as I live, saith the Lord, as ye have SPOKEN in mine ears, so will I DO TO YOU"* (Numbers 14:28).

When you declare God's word, He nods in agreement. He says, "Yes, yes, that's My word, which cannot be broken. O.K. angels, go to work." That was the case with Hezekiah. Isaiah the prophet came to him and said: "Set thine house in order: for thou shalt die, and not live." Hezekiah thought fast, saying, *"I shall go to the gates of the grave: I am deprived of the residue of my years."* So he turned his face to the wall and cried out, reminding God of His word. Then God replied through Isaiah immediately, *"Go, and say to Hezekiah, Thus saith the Lord, the God of David thy father, I have heard thy prayer ... behold, I will add unto thy days fifteen years"* (Isaiah 38; 2 Kings 20).

You can commit God by declaring His word. You need not be cast down when others are cast down. Simply say on the contrary that "there is a lifting up." Then God establishes that declaration; and when others are down, you are up!

Angels Are Set To Work

Furthermore, angels are released to work in your

favour when you utter positive words.

"Bless the Lord, ye his angels, that excel in strength, that do his commandments, hearkening to the voice of his word."

Psalms 103:20

Angels are ministering spirits sent to minister for us who are heirs of salvation. Though they are assigned to you, they work on instructions from you. As a matter of fact, you cannot say before an angel, *"It was an error" (Ecclesiastes 5:6).* Meaning they obey the last command.

If you say you're weak, they organize weakness for you. If you say you're strong, they ensure that you remain strong. Even when in confidence you tell a close friend that you are weak, they hear you, because as spirit beings they are everywhere. Remember that they are on special assignment to you. As a result, they cannot let you out of their sight, otherwise they stand to be queried by God. Even in the secret place, speak right words. As you do, you are operating the spirit of faith.

"But what saith it? The word is nigh thee, even in thy mouth and in thy heart: that is, the word of faith, which we preach."

Romans 10:8

39

It is a thought of faith until it is released from your mouth. Then it becomes a word of faith. This word is a hammer that breaks up your fallow grounds. It is also like fire, that burns up the things you don't want (Luke 21:15). So, use it positively.

Three

How it Operates

"Yea, a man may say, Thou hast faith, and I have works: shew me thy faith without thy works, and I will shew thee my faith by my works."

James 2:18

"How then does faith work?" might be the next question on your mind. Read this sister's testimony, shared before the assembly of God's people.

"I lost my first pregnancy, and for one year, I kept lactating; the milk won't stop coming! No drug could help; neither was any pregnancy coming forth, for one year going to two years. During one of the services last year, the Bishop asked every woman desiring the fruit of the womb to come out and carry the baby of a woman who had her baby after five years. He also told us to go announcing to everyone we saw that we were pregnant. And in October 1993, I got pregnant, still lactating! The bouncing baby boy was born on my husband's birthday. He was my birthday present to him."

How do you explain that, except that with God all things are possible! God's servant had called all those expecting the fruit of the womb to come out. This sister stepped out. He asked them to carry the baby of a sister who had received a baby after waiting for five years, and she did as instructed. Then the Bishop announced, *"Go announce to everyone you see that you are pregnant."* This sister again did as commanded.

Perhaps there were several others in the congregation that day, who heard the call for women in that category and refused to step out. Perhaps also among those who stepped out were one or two who did not carry the miracle baby, saying, *"Where is it written in the Bible that you must carry someone else's baby to receive yours?"* Perhaps some passed the first two tests, but felt ashamed to announce to everyone they met that they had conceived, thinking, *"What if I say it and it doesn't materialize?"* Like Naaman, some times, except you follow divine instructions to the letter, the desired result doesn't come. This is a practical demonstration of how the spirit of faith operates.

Operating the spirit of faith entails acting on what you believe. For instance, 3 John 2 declares that God's wish is that you prosper. But until you start doing something about 3 John 2, prosperity remains only a wish in God's heart. As the saying goes, *"If wishes were horses beggars would ride."* (Only beggars ride on wishes, serious men do something about what they believe). When you give, you have an opportunity to receive, which culminates in financial prosperity.

Many years ago, when we had only one car (a Mercedes Benz), God spoke to my husband to sell it and give the proceeds to expand the ministry of some missionaries in Northern Nigeria. We gladly gave the car, and today we are overjoyed to see these ministries expanding to the glory of God. We also have received many more cars entrusted to us by the Lord, and financially we are prospering.

ACT ON WHAT YOU BELIEVE

Dr. Frederick K. C. Price, in his book, *"How faith*

Works", gives an illustration to explain the difference between belief and faith. It goes like this:

"A man staggers through the door .... over to a chair ... prepares to sit down at a table .... but instead, he falls onto the floor.

Several people rush to his side ...They pick him up ... and set him in the chair. He seems to have passed out. They fan him ... wake him up... and say, "Brother, what's the matter? What's the matter with you?"

Groggily and weakly he answers, "Ah ... I don't know. I don't know." Somebody says, "I wonder if there's a doctor in this motel?" The group calls the desk. Sure enough there happens to be a doctor in the motel. The doctor enters and makes a preliminary examination of the man.

THE DOCTOR: "This man is in the final stages of starvation. This man is suffering from malnutrition. He's almost dead. Given another 30 minutes - all things being equal - this man will be dead. He's starving to death." The leaders get together and say, "Let's go down to the kitchen and see if we can get the chef to prepare some food for this man. We certainly don't want him to starve to death."

They enter later with a four-wheeler, loaded down with all kinds of good food. They wheel it up to the man and say, "Brother, do you see this food?" And He says, "Oh, yes." They say again, "Do you believe that if you eat this food it will keep you from starving to death?" And again, he says, "Oh, yes, certainly I believe that if I eat this food it will keep me from starving to death."

Then he says it again, "I believe that if I eat this food it will keep me from starving to death ... I believe that if I eat this food it will keep me from starving to death."

(Now remember, the doctor had given him 30 minutes to live).

So ... 29 minutes and 50 seconds later... the man is heard to say, "I believe that if I eat this food it will keep me from starving to death ..." He falls to the floor. The doctor rushes to his side and says, "This man is dead."

The man believed absolutely that by eating the food it would keep him from starving to death, yet he died. Why? Because although he claimed to believe, he did nothing about what he believed - he didn't eat the food!

Many in the Body of Christ today, who are suffering from sickness, poverty, failure and depression, believe the word of God. They believe the Bible holds the keys to opening up the doors to divine health, financial prosperity, success and joy unspeakable; yet they live poor, defeated lives. Why? No corresponding action to show what they claim to believe, which is a vital step in operating the spirit of faith. The Bible calls something self deceit: when you hear the word, give it mental accent, yet refuse to do what it requires of you.

> *"But be ye doers of the word, and not hearers only, deceiving your own selves."*
>
> James 1:22

Why is it easier to believe the word of a man than it is to believe that of the Almighty God? Some one promises you a job, calls you in for an interview and offers you a mouth-watering salary. Whether you have seen his account or not to verify that the said amount exists, you begin to announce to everyone what your new pay packet is. You may even buy some new clothes on credit saying, "I'll pay you at the end of the month."

Upon what is your faith founded? It's founded upon the integrity of the man and his word. If the man is a man of his word, then at the end of the month he cannot say, "There's no more money in the account."

Similarly, your faith in God is founded upon the character of God and upon His word. You know He cannot lie (Titus 1:2); whatever He says, therefore, is the truth. You know He cannot change and cannot fail, so you should have absolute confidence in His word, even more than you have confidence in your doctor and his diagnosis.

God is Jehovah-Ropheka, our Healer. He is the "manufacturer" of the human body, so you can expect Him to have spare parts; and to be able to repair any damaged organ. Thus you can put your faith in Him. Instead of putting your faith in the doctors' report or peoples' report, let your faith be in God's report. Believe His Word and act on it. It works!

Dr. T. L. Osborn defines faith as: "You are convinced that what God promised, and what you asked for is yours; that you have received it, even before you can see or feel it. That faith is based on God's promise alone.

An instance is when you pray for healing, but the answer is not instantly manifested. You may still feel the pain, but God's Word declares that *by His Stripes you were healed.* Your mind tells you the sickness is still there, but you must abandon your reasoning and believe God's Word. Pay attention to the word, not to what you see or feel."

"For we walk by faith, not by sight."
II Corinthians 5:7

47

Genuine faith always declares thus:

"God is who He says He is!

I am what God's word says I am!

I can do what He says I can do!

God will do what His word says He will do!"

Yet faith without works is dead.

"What doth it profit, my brethren, though a man say he have faith, and have not works? Can faith save him? Thou believest that there is one God; thou doest well: the devils also believe and tremble.

But wilt thou know, O vain man, that faith without works is dead?"

James 2:14,19,20

Add action, therefore, to your belief. It's the only genuine proof of your belief.

Four

Now Faith is...

Faith, according to Hebrews 11:1, is, *"the substance of things hoped for; the evidence of things not seen."* Faith is two things as described above: it is a substance, and also an evidence or proof. It is a tangible substance, belonging to the unseen realm. You cannot see faith with your physical eyes, [it's not like your Bible which you can see before you, for instance], but you can perceive faith with your spiritual senses.

For instance, someone promises you a few thousands of naira. You have not yet received the money, so you hold on to his promise. If anyone asks you your financial condition, you may say, "Man, I am very rich!"

You are holding onto the promise of that person. Monday morning, he calls you and hands over the money to you. Now you are holding the physical cash, no longer the mere promise. If anyone asks you your financial state, you can boldly declare, "I have a few thousands of Naira." The answer replaces the promise.

However, even before the man gives you the money, you already walk like you have the money in your bank account. You go around pricing bags of rice and electronic gadgets, not because you have received it physically, but because you believe the person who made the promise to you.

That was exactly the case with Abraham and Sarah. They were still very barren, yet they were already calling themselves *"Father and Mother of many nations."* By accepting the change in name, Abraham proved that he believed God would fulfill His promise. Perhaps they had already bought their baby clothes, baby cot, etc. All in faith. Somebody asks, *"What were they holding onto for the twenty-five years they waited?"* The promise of God (Romans 4:20-21). When Isaac came, they held Isaac. But before he came, they held on to their faith.

Faith is what gives your hope substance. For instance, God's Word declares that you shall lend to nations, and not borrow. You hope for that to be accomplished. For you, it may still be for a time to come. That's hope. But hope has no substance, no tangibility. You can keep hoping and never arrive at anything until faith is added to it. Faith is like the petrol that makes the car of hope work. The difference between hope and faith is that faith is in the "now". Hope is tomorrow. Hope said: *"I believe I will be healed someday."* Faith says: "Inspite of the symptoms, I know I am healed; because He took my infirmities and bore my sicknesses, and by His stripes I am healed." At this point, you have not yet seen a physical manifestation of your healing, so you're hoping for it; but you believe God's word, so you declare those things which *"be not as though they were."* That is, adding faith to your hope and it always works.

That is why, although you hope to lend to nations someday, you begin declaring right now that *"you are the head and cannot be the tail; you are above and cannot be beneath. You are a lender (to nations) and not a borrower."* As further proof that you have faith in that Word you begin to give. You pay your tithes, give offerings, invest in the kingdom, etc. You are giving substance to your hope.

A woman shared a moving testimony in our church.

Her sister had been married for over twenty years without a child (she was almost becoming another Sarah). She had hoped and hoped for twenty years without success. As a member of the church, her sister came to service one day burdened with this issue. As she approached the entrance of the church, the enemy taunted her saying, "Cannot this God whom you have been serving bless your sister with a child?" Refusing to give heed to the devil's mockery, and rejecting depression, she said, "I will still serve God inspite of the circumstance." Adding faith to her hope, she stood in for her sister when prayer was made for barren women. She then ran to her sister's house, found her and declared: "This month you shall be pregnant." Without any argument her sister received the word, and that same month, the twenty years reproach was rolled away and she conceived! At the time this testimony was shared the child was about five months old! God can turn impossible situations around for those who possess the spirit of faith!

Faith is also the evidence of things not seen. What are the things you are desirous of? I have good news for you. God also wants you to have them.

*"Therefore I say unto you, What **things** soever ye*

desire, when you pray, believe that ye receive them, and ye shall have them."

Mark 11:24

Those spiritual or material things you desire to have from God, but do not have at the moment, you can be assured that they will soon be in your possession. How? By faith, because you have faith that having asked them of God they are on the way. Somebody may ask you: "If you really know that those things are yours, show me an evidence of it or prove it." You then reply, "God said it is mine in His word, and I have faith in His word. So my evidence is my faith in His word."

Although you have not seen or received your desire, you can declare in faith that what you desire is yours. The word "evidence" means "that which supports the fact that a thing exists." In the court of law, the lawyer must produce an evidence to support the facts that he is presenting. If he claims that his client is not guilty, he must present evidences or proofs.

Are you healed of your diseases? Where is your evidence? You may still feel the symptoms, but if you are to exercise faith, inspite of what is seen, you must search out the Word of God and hold on to it as the evidence of your healing. The world, the flesh, and the devil, like the judge in the court of law, ask you always to produce an evidence that you are healed, rich, or successful. Your faith in the Word is your evidence. It is the evidence of what you believe but have not seen. All that you desire is available in the realm of the unseen - that new car, that house, promotion at your work, healing, etc. have been released to you.

> **"Blessed be the God and Father of our Lord Jesus Christ, who hath blessed us with all spiritual blessings in heavenly places in Christ."**
>
> Ephesians 1:3

All you need do is search out the promises of God that makes them yours, and by faith receive them. For instance, your aunt in London instructs her bank to transfer five thousand pounds into your bank account in Kaduna. She then calls you on phone to inform you of what she has done. Do you wait until the money arrives to say "thank you"? No! Right away you thank her for the kind gesture. You then drop the receiver and jump, shouting, "Halleluia! I <u>have</u> five thousand pounds!" You begin to inform everyone around the house that you have five thousand pounds. You may even share the testimony before God's people, all the while saying, "I have." That's natural faith. Spiritual faith works the same way.

The money has not yet been transferred into your account; your aunt only called to inform you that she has instructed her bank to transfer that amount to you. You don't even use the future tense to indicate that it is an event of the future. You use the present tense "I have". Why? You know your aunt has the money. In other words, she has the ability. Secondly, you believe that when she promises a thing she will fulfill it (perhaps she has fulfilled several other promises before). Thus your faith is based on her word.

If she never called you on phone and you never heard from her you wouldn't have cause to exercise faith. So then, faith comes by words (whether spoken or written). If someone was to ask you to prove that you have five thousand pounds, you would simply laugh and say, "I know who my aunt is. She doesn't play with words. When she promises, she fulfills her promise!"

This illustration should help you understand why Paul could say:

"... For I know whom I have believed [trusted], and am persuaded that he is able to keep that which I have committed unto him against that day."

II Timothy 1:12

Do you know in whom you are trusting? Are you persuaded that He is able to do exceedingly abundantly more than you ask or think? That is faith. There is a difference between faith and mental assent. Mental assent may not be based on God's promise, and does not produce corresponding action. Your action must be in line with your faith for it to be productive.

FAITH IS ... "AT THY WORD"

> *"Now when he had left speaking, he said unto Simon, Launch out into the deep, and let down your nets for a draught.*
>
> *And Simon answering said unto him, Master, we have toiled all the night, and have taken nothing: <u>nevertheless at thy word</u> I will let down the net.*
>
> *And when they had this done, they enclosed a great multitude of fishes: and their net brake."*
>
> Luke 5:4-6

Peter would have missed catching a great multitude of fishes if he had said, "You are just a carpenter, we are trained fishermen, and have a lot of experience. If anyone should know where the fishes are, when to fish, and how to catch them, we should, not you." No! Rather, he agreed with Jesus, and acted on His Word. It was at that point that his toiling ceased and he began to have results.

Many times God's Word will tell you to do what seems ridiculous in the natural; things that defy logic. Yet it is in the doing of it that the miraculous appears. Let me share this testimony of a sister with you:

"When I gave birth to my baby, she had a lump on her head, behind her right ear. I took her to the hospital and the doctors said she would need to be operated upon, to remove the lump. They, however, also said not many babies survive the operation, but that I should go and prepare for the operation all the same. When I got home, my husband said I should wait and not do the operation yet, and I agreed with him.

But this morning, when the Bishop said we should stand up and begin to rejoice with all our might, that something was going to happen in our lives today, I immediately stood up, anointed the lump, and began to strike it with my mantle (prayer cloth), dancing and shouting. And when I touched the place again, there was nothing there! It was gone!"

This wise woman gave heed to the instruction of the man of God, and a lump that could have terminated the life of that child disappeared. You have argued enough, now act on the Word! You have narrated your plight to everyone who cares to listen enough;

now act on the Word! You have claimed to be relying on the Word of God for a job, whereas you are relying on your wealthy uncle for a job. Now stand on the Word, believe God has released it to you according to your desire, and go for that job. Rise up early when others rise up to go to work, dress up too, and move out.

An unemployed brother testified that after receiving a message of this sort in church he rose up early, put on his suit and headed for the post-office (by divine inspiration). At the post-office he heard two people discussing the venue of an interview. He quickly went there and was the candidate employed! Your success story will be the next one!

No matter for how long you have toiled, until you act on His Word, the struggle continues. Stand on the Word, in your family life, business, ministry, etc. That's faith!

Five

Activating the Spirit of Faith

"For by grace are ye saved through faith; and that not of yourselves, it is the gift of God."

Ephesians 2:8

You are saved because of the grace of God, and also by the exercise of your faith in that grace (Romans 10:9,10). You believe in your heart and confess Jesus with your mouth. That's a step of faith. Anyone who asks how it is possible cannot be born again. Why?

He must believe that He is who He says He is, and that He exists and is a rewarder of all them that diligently seek him (Hebrews 11:6). He must believe in the invisible God and act out his believing by opening up his mouth and making a confession of faith.

The Christian walk is one of faith. Therefore, you must cry out for the spirit of faith to fill you up to the brim; for it is the spirit of faith that helps you believe for the extraordinary and miraculous. It helps you take giant strides in God and for Christ. It enables you establish the victory of Christ in your life (I John 5:14).

God desires you to experience the miraculous on a daily basis. His desire for you is to enjoy victory over satanic oppression and all life's situations. But to do so, the spirit of faith must be in constant and daily operation in your life. You may ask how can it be done? By activating it!

Activating or activation means to accelerate an occurrence. You need to accelerate your operation of the spirit of faith daily; and then you will find the miraculous a daily occurrence for you.

THE KEY OF KNOWLEDGE

"According to his divine power hath given unto us

all things that pertain unto life and godliness, through the <u>KNOWLEDGE</u> of him that hath called us to glory and virtue."

2 Peter 1:3

The simple fact that you are born of God does not guarantee you victory. To overcome, you need to operate in faith, and faith comes via what you know, i.e. knowledge. If you discover who you are in Christ, you won't be toyed with by sickness, disease, armed robbers, witches or wizards. You will overcome all these by the exercise of your faith. However, it is important for you to know what God has said about you as a child of God, and what His provisions are for your fulfillment on earth.

I remember what happened when I was pregnant with our first son, David. One day I saw blood flowing from me. Medically, such a situation is pronounced by doctors as a miscarriage. Not long after, my husband returned home from an outside engagement, and I told him that I had had a miscarriage. Boldly, and without any hesitation, he said, "You can't have a miscarriage", and then asked to be served his meal.

That statement activated the spirit of faith and ended any further discussion on the matter; and the pregnancy was sustained. He attended a prayer meeting that same day, undisturbed by what I had said. What gave him that boldness? What made the spirit of faith flow easily from him? The knowledge of God's Word in Exodus 23:25-26 (TLB), which says:

> *"You shall serve the Lord your God only; then I will bless you with food and with water, and I will take away sickness from among you. There will be no miscarriages nor barrenness throughout your land ..."*

He knew who had made this promise, and that he had fulfilled the condition of service to the Lord. So he was confident that I couldn't have a miscarriage or be barren. His words that day transmitted the spirit of faith into me, and I had a smooth delivery of our son. Ignorance could have caused fear to gain a place in our hearts and we would have eventually lost the pregnancy. But knowledge activates and stirs up the spirit of faith into operation in your life.

> *"Seek ye out of the book of the Lord, and read: no one of these shall fail ..."*
>
> Isaiah 34:16

Making a qualitative search of the scriptures and Christian literature is a sure way of increasing your knowledge of God's promises to you. The scripture says when you locate the promise, it won't fail you;

and as long as your faith is in proper place it will pro-duce for you.

TAKE HEED HOW YE HEAR

In Acts 14, a man crippled from his mother's womb received his miracle in Lystra, because Paul perceived the man had faith to be healed.

> *"The <u>same heard Paul speak</u>: who stedfastly beholding him, <u>and perceiving that he had faith to be healed,</u> Said with a loud voice, Stand upright on thy feet. And he leaped and walked."*
>
> *Acts 14:9,10*

The healing of this man followed a pattern. First, he heard Paul speak (faith comes by the hearing of the Word of God - Romans 10:17). Then he believed in what Paul was saying; and because he was open to those words, the spirit behind the words entered into him *(Ezekiel 2:2)*. When Paul commanded, *"Stand upright on thy feet"*, the man could not see any changes in his physical condition. As far as he could see, he was still as lame as when he was born, yet he acted on what he believed, and by the spirit that had entered into him, he leaped up. It was not until he took that leap of faith that healing came, and he was able to walk.

"Faith cometh by <u>hearing</u> and hearing by the Word of God."

Romans 10:17

Therefore, listening to the Word of God being taught activates the spirit of faith in you. Jesus Himself declares, *"... The words that I speak unto you they are <u>spirit</u>, and they are <u>life</u>" (John 6:63).*

As the spoken Words come forth, they are able to stir up your faith just as Paul's words stirred up the faith of that man at Lystra. The spirit of faith is transmitted through the spoken words. Care must, therefore, be taken not to entertain or give heed to what is contrary to faith or your expected desire. No wonder Jesus warned:

"Take heed what ye hear: with <u>what measure ye mete, it shall be measured to you</u>: and unto you that hear shall more be given."

Mark 4:24

The Amplified Bible renders it beautifully: *"The measure [of thought and study] you give [to the truth you hear] will be the measure [of virtue and knowledge] that comes back to you."* What do knowledge and virtue do? They stir up your faith. The time you give to hear God's Word, good reports, and testimonies is never wasted.

I am privileged to be married to a man who operates the spirit of faith regularly. I remember a day in 1983; I went to the bathroom to have a shower and discovered that the soap was almost finished. I went to my husband and said, "The soap in the bathroom is the last one." Those were the days when basic necessities were rationed. In those days, even if you had the money, you could not find basic essentials like soap or milk to buy. We had to line up for virtually everything. So I said, "This soap in the bathroom is the last one." He said to me "No! that cannot be the last soap." I said, "Okay", because the words he spoke activated the spirit of faith in me.

Later, he gave the brother living with us some money to buy soap on his way back from school. Truly, the brother returned with bars of soap and several other things, explaining that mysteriously, a van came to their school for the first time to sell essential commodities; something that had never happened before! Then I understood that we could not have lacked, even if the whole country was in lack. We who operate in the spirit of faith should not experience what others are experiencing. As we believed and took a step of faith by giving the young man money to buy soap, God saw to it that our desire was granted.

DECLARE YOUR DESIRE WITH THANKSGIVING

Thanksgiving is a vital part of faith. When you believe something has been given to you, what do you say? "Thank you." Even before you see and feel the answer, thank God!

Hope believes the blessing will come someday. The senses believe when it feels healed. Faith on the other hand believes it has the thing that is desired now, because the Word says so. Faith calls the things which be not as though they were (Romans 4:17). Jesus was an expert at this. He always spoke in the past tense.

"Father, I thank thee that thou <u>hast heard</u> me."
John 11:41

"... Take heed what ye hear: with <u>what measure ye mete, it shall be measured to you</u>: and unto you that hear shall more be given."

Mark 4:24

Lazarus was dead and already stinking, yet Jesus called those things which be not, as though they were. He believed He had received while He prayed, and it was so. Faith for healing works the same way as faith for salvation and faith for provision. You must believe first, and then confess. Haven't you seen sincere

Christians who die prematurely, all because they were "closed-mouthed" Christians? You are an overcomer only as you declare what God's Word says about you.

As you thank Him, declaring His faithfulness, begin to do the things you couldn't do before. After a church service in which a sister, in obedience to the Lord, gave all she had, she returned home and found she had absolutely nothing to present to her family for dinner. Rather than accuse God, complain or bombard heaven, she told her children to set the table and served water as food. Her family members were all believers, so they raised up their voices in thanksgiving to God, confident that He supplies all needs. They dialed heavens hot line: "Father, we thank you."

Just as God moved rapidly to multiply the loaves and fishes for Jesus when He gave thanks, angels were immediately sent into action. By the following morning, a man came from no where and said, "God said I should bring this to you." When they opened it, it was four thousand naira! Without a doubt, God is Jehovah Jireh, who supplies all our needs according to His riches in glory, when we believe His Word and speak accordingly.

My husband often says, "Don't tell trials, tell testimonies." Declare with thanks the good things that have happened and will happen to you, refuse to dwell on or declare the negative. When David was faced with the challenge of defeating Goliath, he did not magnify Goliath's size or his weapons. Rather, he declared how God had helped him in the past to kill a lion and a bear, and how the same God would help him defeat Goliath. David had exactly what he said (I Samuel 17:36)!

Six

YOUR FUTURE IS BRIGHT!

"And it shall come to pass in the last days, that the mountain of the Lord's house shall be established in the top of the mountains, and shall be exalted above the hills; and all nations shall flow unto it.

And many people shall go and say, Come ye, and let us go up to the mountain of the Lord, to the house of the God of Jacob; and he will teach us of his ways, and we will walk in his paths: for out of Zion shall go forth the law, and the word of the Lord from Jerusalem."

Isaiah 2:2,3

These are the last days. They are days of mourning

for the world, but days of glory for Zion. Amidst all the rumours of wars and actual wars, for you it will be rumours of promotion and actual promotions! Amidst the famine in nations of the world, you who fear the Lord will eat in plenty and be satisfied, and praise the name of the Lord your God. While businesses are crashing, yours will be cruising on higher altitudes; and because the higher you go the cooler it becomes, instead of experiencing the financial and economic heat the rest of the world is facing, you will only see it with your eyes, but it will not be your portion.

This is God's agenda for you. It is no gimmick by positive thinkers and escapists, to make you feel good, but the actual will of God for you. As the Church is lifted and established as the most successful institution in the whole world, you who make up the Church will also be lifted and be established. You will be on top always and be exalted above your equals (and seniors). For instance, when a man is exalted and made the Minister of Defense, all members of his family are automatically lifted. They live in a government provided house, have cars and drivers, cooks and stewards - all coming with the new appointment.

Now our Senior Brother, Jesus, is lifted. He is seated at the right hand of majesty, next to God the Father.

Those of us who are members of His family are also exalted, seated with Him in heavenly places, far above principalities and powers. Not only that, we are also members of His body. Therefore, as the body is exalted, whether you're a toenail or a strand of hair on the leg, you too are exalted!

My husband shared a testimony of a 24 year old in America, who was sent out of school because he could not make up his grades. He was an engineering student. Although he was sent out of school, God gave him a unique insight into manufacturing a certain computer hardware. When the product came into the market, it fetched him 400 million dollars. He was branded a failure, but he rejected it and went ahead to prove them wrong. Your future is bright! Others may call you a failure, but it is what God calls you that counts. He has said you are the head; agree with Him.

All you need to make it in life is in you. But until you activate it, failure will keep staring you in the face. What are you desirous of? Your future is bright! As long as you are joined to Jesus, the Vine, no issue of your life is hopeless. Because He lives, you must live also. Jesus is successful, so you too must be successful. He is healthy, you must be healthy too.

This goes for victory, prosperity, and greatness. All you must ascertain is that you are properly connected to Him.

> *"I am the vine, ye are the branches: He that abideth in me, and I in him, the same bringeth forth much fruit: for without me ye can do nothing."*
>
> John 15:5

If without Him you can do nothing, with Him therefore, you can do all things. With the spirit of faith operating in you, you can do all things. You can become a Joshua, that caused the sun and moon to stand still.

Abraham stayed with God until he received his expectation. He *"against hope believed in hope."* Stop looking at your present situation, let your eyes be fixed, trusting in the Lord. When you permit the spirit of faith to work in you, you will have no cause to stagger in unbelief. God is glorified when you are strong in faith, and will send your answer speedily (Romans 4:17-20).

Stop considering the doctors' reports. You are healed! Your future is bright! You can live a healthy life by faith. You can live till you are 120 years old, without your eyes growing dim or your natural force slackening like Moses' - all by faith. If you want to please God, then you must choose the life of faith.

Stop reading the economic analysts' report; your business will prosper, your future is bright! Stop counting how many marriages have broken; yours cannot break, your future is bright!

The reason we have arrived at the point we are in Christ today is because right from the time when nothing seemed glorious, we saw our future as glorious, enviable, and bright. What do you see?

> *"... Lift up now thine eyes, and look from the place where thou art northward, and southward, and eastward and westward:*
>
> *For all the land which thou seest, to thee will I give it, and to thy seed for ever."*
>
> Genesis 13:14,15

See that glorious tomorrow and celebrate it today. Those who can see their tomorrow cannot get arrested by present circumstances. Let what you see drive you to success. You don't need to rely on any man.

Time and time again my husband and I have witnessed the results of operating in the spirit of faith. In the work of the ministry that we are privileged to be involved in, the spirit of faith has been our companion. For as God has revealed each step we were to take, the spirit of faith energizes us to keep going forward, obeying and doing as God has commanded us to, even when there was nothing visible to make us believe it. Now God has done it! He has made us living proofs. He can do the same for you too!